بِسْمِ اللهِ الرَّحْمٰنِ الرَّحِيمِ

In the name of Allah, The All-Merciful,
The Kindest towards believers.

Disclaimer

All rights reserved. No part of this publication may be reproduced, stored in a retrieval system, or transmitted in any form or by any means, electronic, mechanical, photocopying, recording, or otherwise, without the prior written permission of the publisher, except in the case of brief quotations quoted in articles or reviews.

Contact : Admin@islamiclessonsmadeeasy.com.au

Visit us :
- Facebook.com/islamiclessonsmadeeasy
- Youtube.com/islamiclessonsmadeeasy
- Instagram.com/islamic_lessons_me
- Islamiclessonsmadeeasy.com.au
- Ilme.net.au

The pictures used are the property of Islamic Lessons Made Easy. The content and rulings are taken from various leading scholars and are presented in a simplified manner. Therefore, for the exact definition and explanation, please refer to the original sources.

First Edition
©Copyright 2024 Islamic Lessons Made Easy

Transliteration

Arabic	Translit.	Arabic	Translit.
ا	a	ق	q
ب	b	ك	k
ت	t	ل	l
ث	th	م	m
ج	j	ن	n
ح	ḥ	ه	h
خ	kh	و	w
د	d	ي	y
ذ	dh	ـَا / ئ / آ	ā
ر	r	ـِي	ī
ز	z	ـُو	ū
س	s		
ش	sh		
ص	ṣ		
ض	ḍ		
ط	ṭ		
ظ	ẓ		
ع	ʿ		
غ	gh		
ف	f		

ʾ - Read with a sudden pause of air.

(saw) - Blessings of Allah be upon him and his family.

(n) - Better not to pronounce it. But if you do pronounce it, you do not pronounce the letter after it.

(as) - Peace be upon him/them.

(swt) - Glorious and Exalted Is He.

When entering toilet

When looking in a mirror

When exiting toilet

أَلْحَمْدُ لِلهِ الَّذِي كَسَانِي مَا يُوَارِي عَوْرَتِي وَأَتَجَمَّلُ بِهِ فِي النَّاسِ

Alḥamdu lil lāhil-ladhī kasānī mā yuwārī 'awratī wa a-tajammalu bihi fin nās

Praise be to Allah who clothed me with what covers my nakedness and with what I adorn myself among the people.

When wearing clothes

بِسْمِ اللهِ، بَارِكْ لَنَا فِيمَا رَزَقْتَنَا وَعَلَيْكَ خَلْفَهُ

Bismillāh, bārik lanā fīmā razaqtanā wa ʿalayka khalfah

In the name of Allah, bless for us from what you have given us of sustenance and upon You do we rely for its replenishment.

After you eat

اَلْحَمْدُ لِلّٰهِ الَّذِيْ اَطْعَمَنَا، وَسَقَانَا، وَكَفَانَا، وَاَيَّدَنَا، وَآوَانَا، وَاَنْعَمَ عَلَيْنَا، وَاَفْضَلَ. اَلْحَمْدُ لِلّٰهِ الَّذِيْ يُطْعِمُ وَلاَ يُطْعَمُ

Alḥamdu lil lāhil-ladhī aṭʿamanā, wa saqānā, wa kafānā, wa ayyadanā, wa āwānā, wa anʿama ʿalaynā, wa afḍal. Alḥamdu lil lāhil-ladhī yuṭʿimu wa lā yuṭʿam

Praise be to Allah Who has: fed us, provided water for us, sufficed us, supported us, sheltered us, favored us, and bestowed benefits. Praise be to Allah Who feeds but is not fed.

When drinking water

أَلْحَمْدُ لِلهِ الَّذِي لَمْ يَجْعَلْهُ أُجَاجاً بِذُنُوبِنَا وَ جَعَلَهُ عَذْباً فُرَاتاً بِنِعْمَتِهِ

Alḥamdu lil lāhil-ladhī lam yajʿalhu ujājān bi dhunūbinā wa jaʿalahu ʿadhban furātan bi niʿmatih

All praise be to Allah, the One who did not make this water bitter as a punishment for our sins, and made it sweet and quenching by His grace.

When leaving the house

When entering a mosque

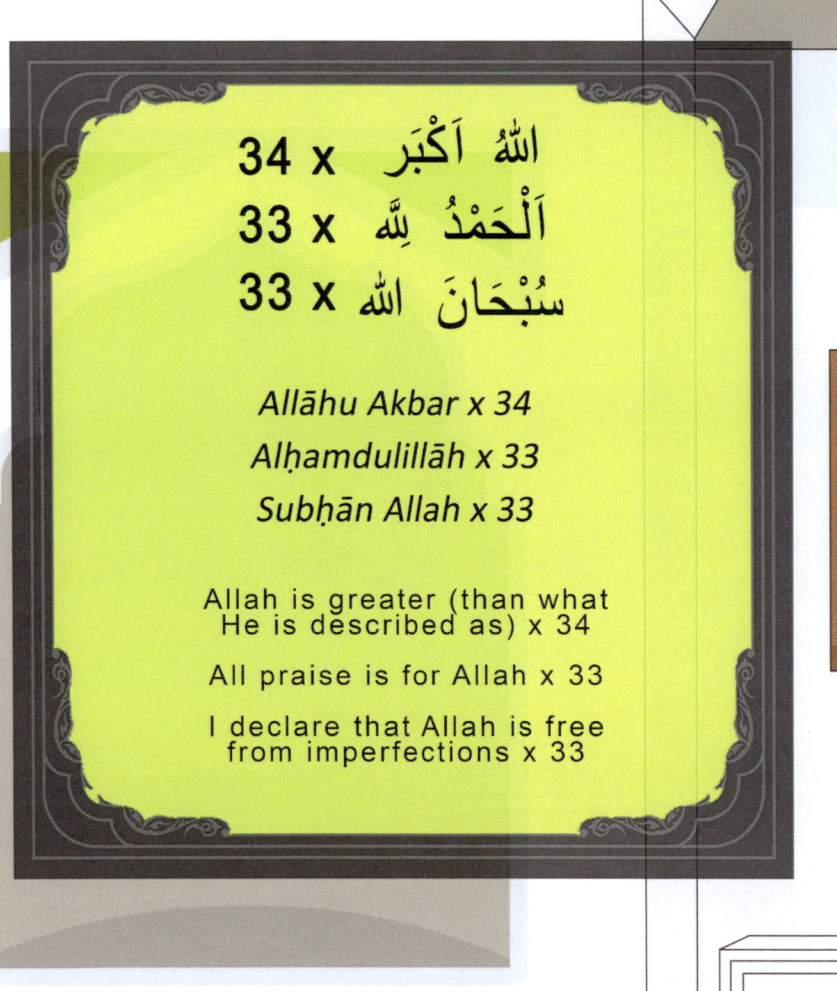

After every prayer

اَللَّهُمَّ افْتَحْ لِي أَبْوَابَ رِزْقِكَ

Allahumma iftaḥ lī abwāba rizqik

O Allah, Open for me the doors of Your Sustenance.

When leaving a mosque

When greeting someone

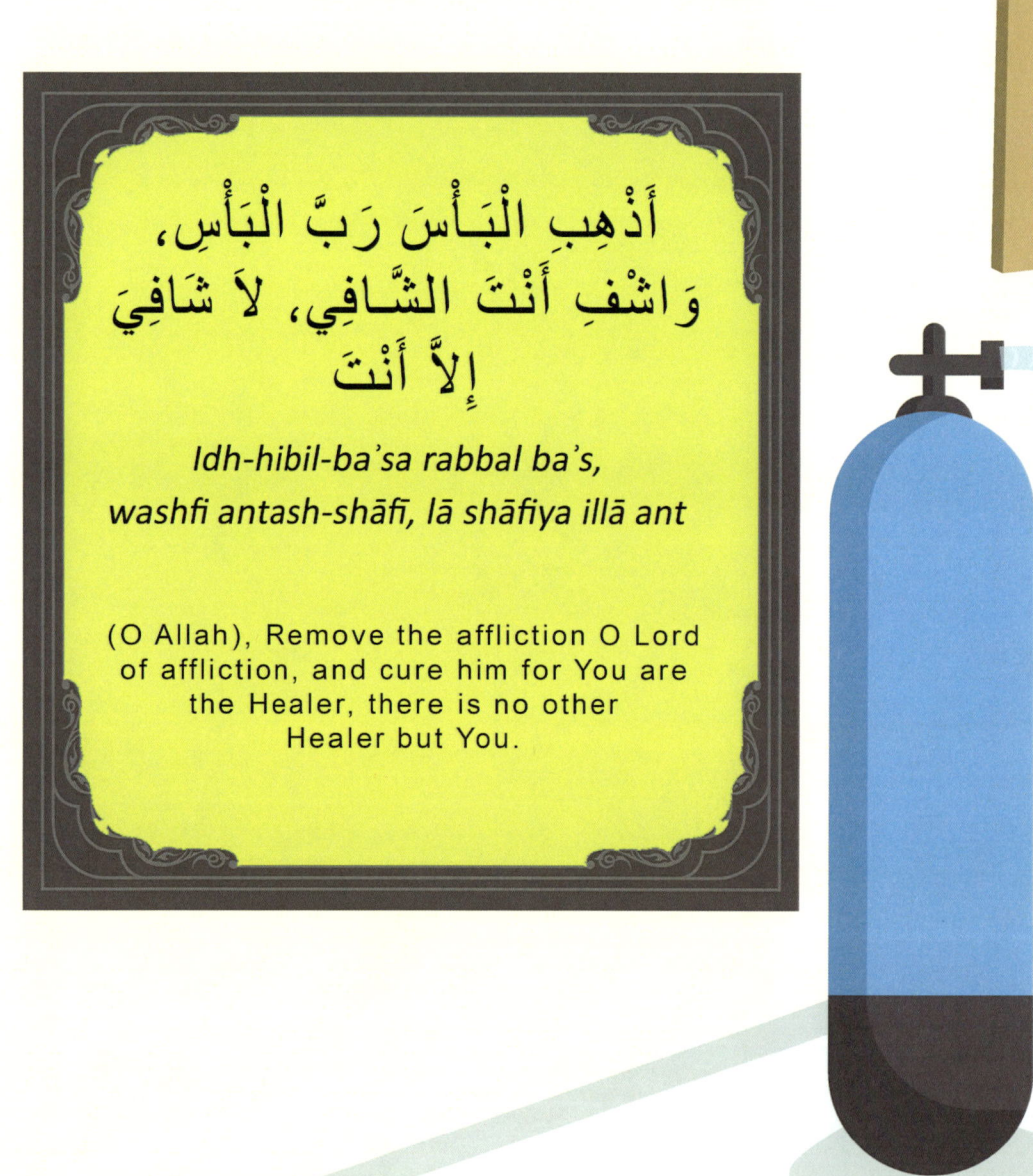

أَذْهِبِ الْبَأْسَ رَبَّ الْبَأْسِ، وَاشْفِ أَنْتَ الشَّافِي، لاَ شَافِيَ إِلاَّ أَنْتَ

Idh-hibil-ba'sa rabbal ba's, washfi antash-shāfī, lā shāfiya illā ant

(O Allah), Remove the affliction O Lord of affliction, and cure him for You are the Healer, there is no other Healer but You.

When visiting a sick person

When sneezing

Before learning

When visiting the graveyard

For condolences

آجَرَكُمُ اللهُ وَرَحِمَكُمْ

Ājarakumul lāhu wa raḥimakum

May Allah recompense you and have mercy on you.

When entering your home

Before sleeping

www.ingramcontent.com/pod-product-compliance
Lightning Source LLC
Chambersburg PA
CBRC091202070526
44583CB00008B/177